RHYTHMIC REFLECTIONS ON LIFE

By Mark J. Spanbauer

Photographs by Amanda J. Ruby

Rhythmic Reflections on Life

Poems Written by Mark Spanbauer

Cover & Interior Photographs by Amanda J. Ruby
Layout & Design by Michael Nicloy

ISBN: 978-1945907449

Published by Nico 11 Publishing & Design
www.nico11publishing.com

Be well read.

Quantity purchase requests can be emailed to:
mike@nico11publishing.com

FOREWORD

RHYTHMIC REFLECTIONS ON LIFE is a collection of short poetic stories that I have written over the past 10 years. Over that time period I had thought deeply about the many aspects of life that I had experienced, seen others experience, or imagined. The first poem in my book titled "Time" came to me as I thought about how our lives, just like the seasons each year, have a start and an end. If we are lucky enough to get to experience a full life, then our lives, just like the seasons, move on and on until they end. My poems "Heaven" and "Inside My Dream" were the direct result of dreams I had. Each dream came to me so I basically woke up and wrote what I saw after each dream. Both dreams were quite vivid so it was easy to put them to words. I have great respect for our country's Military Veterans and for those who gave their lives for our freedom. Some of my poems reflect my gratitude to those who served and I consider my poem "Courage" to be one of my finest efforts. Some of the writings in this book, unfortunately, are of individuals who passed away far too early and never got to experience a full life. May they rest in peace and always be remembered.

Special thanks to my friend Jim Purtell, a decorated Vietnam Combat Medic, and author of the book: *Vietnam; There and Back: A Combat Medic's Chronicle*. "Doc" Purtell gave me valuable advice on making some of my story poems a bit more reader friendly, and I appreciate that he took the time to help me in that regard. I also want to thank my daughter Amanda for the beautiful pictures she took, which are displayed on the cover and interior of my book.

Time

In the spring we crawl, we walk, we run
Always growing and moving ahead
And I guess because we are so young
We look forward to summer instead

And the summer seems to have no end
It's our moment to have fun in the sun
Our friends, our lives and our loves
And we run and we run and we run

Our children they come and then they go
How we love them I hope they know
Like the seasons they move on and on
They too have the need to grow

Now the autumn days are getting cold
And it's time for me and for you
We face the fact that we're getting old
And our best days are almost through

The cold winter seems to have no end
We look back at the good times we had
Our lives just like our favorite song
Are reaching an end and that's oh so sad

But don't be too sad if you have lived a long life
We know of those who never got that chance
Appreciate what you've seen the good and the strife
Those that died young would have loved a longer dance

To The Younger

I want to help and I know it's hard
For you to see things the way I do
But believe it or not there was a time
When I was young and I had troubles too

The young life I knew was not like yours
More difficult times now I have to admit
But you and I have some common things too
Over the years I have learned quite a bit

We also had bullies, there were drugs and alcohol
Our life back then not just a stroll in the sun
We had to study and we had to work
So don't think times back then were all fun

There were days when I also got overwhelmed
A few times thought that I'd reached the end
But thank God that I never took that last step
And because I didn't now please understand

If you get to the point where you want to give up
There are people who want to help you
All you have to do is go ask for some help
Take that step they will help you get through

As time goes on you'll see things differently
You'll be happy with the choices you made
The tough times will fade and you'll realize
You are happy you chose life and you stayed

A Great Generation

They were blessed with great prosperity
After that long and terrible war
They did not rest upon their laurels
For their families they wanted more

Rolled up their sleeves and went to work
Outside their houses; inside their homes
The children knew that they were secure
Because of the love mom and dad had shown

They made America great you know
Our melting pot was forged into steel
The homes they kept; the jobs they did
Our country's greatness they made real

Provided a good home for their children
That pride they all shared; you could see
And showed us the fruits of their labor
Through hard work how good life could be

I lived through those days and those nights
A lucky guy so I know what I'm saying
And because of them we can rest assured
Our Country's anthem will continue playing

Always Near

She thinks about him all the time
So he's never far away
With all the love she has for him
In her heart he'll always stay

And even though he isn't here
His time on earth is now done
Forever in her heart he lives
For he was her only one

She knows some day they'll meet again
And they'll never again have to part
Forever they will live as one
She believes that in her heart

The faith she has will pull her through
As she endures this lonely life
She knows the time will come again
When she'll forever be his wife

America

America where have you gone?
Seems nothing like our favorite song
United we were meant to be
United? Not much of it I see

It's not supposed to be this way
Please tell me what's gone wrong
A melting pot is what they say
So why can't we all get along

It wasn't written up this way
We've dug a hole; is it too late?
Equality for all is what they say
But for many; just fight and hate

Divided we fall divided we fall
There's no sugar coating it at all
America where have you gone?
Seems nothing like our favorite song

Courage

Aboard that ship or in the field
On that aircraft; in that tank
To risk your life the way you did
Every one of you we thank

How did you do the things you did?
Knowing the end was always near
How did you handle all those thoughts?
And deal with all that fear

To those that served and didn't return
I know this much is true
You'll never be forgotten
And our salute goes out to you

And lest we not forget the ones
For the wounded you eased their pain
To see and do the things you did
The horror and the strain

To you that made it back alive
For some it must be tough
How hard it has to be some days
To remember all that stuff

For even though you made it back
Some pain I'm sure you've hid
True heroes every one of you
For everything you did

Breaking Glass

That breaking glass so deafening
As my world crashed all around
I lay awake night after night
Dying from lack of sound

As my heart and body slowly died
I could feel the end was near
So I prayed to God to end my life
But instead I began to hear

And slowly as he spoke to me
I began to feel some light
I slipped back there so many times
But at least I had some fight

So I live my life now day by day
I always try to do my best
To see the good things in my life
And remember how I've been blessed

Still I slip back to that lonely place
Yes that place is still around
That breaking glass so deafening
Dying from lack of sound

Don't Worry

As my mother lay upon the bed
And her life was winding down
I held her hand and whispered
Please don't worry mom don't frown

Since you believe that Jesus died
So that all of us could live
You'll soon be with the ones you love
And feel the comfort they will give

You'll feel a deep enduring love
Warmth like the summer sun
Just like you felt so long ago
Care free days when you were young

And as her eyes were closing
Her frown turned into a smile
And I knew she felt she'd be O.K.
All would be well in a short while

Oh Mentor

You didn't have to take him in
But because you did I can't begin
To tell you it's meant to me
I hope my words can help you see

The lives you've changed by what you did
You brought things out that once were hid
Turned on the lights that once were dim
My son was one you did that for him

For every honor bestowed on you
Please understand this much is true
Your finest honors live and breathe
On Mentor you helped them achieve

Please

I do not want to leave
You know I want to stay
I'll miss holding my kids
I'll miss it every day

But I know it is your will
When it's time for me to go
I'm afraid; I know I shouldn't be
I have to leave them I know it's so

So I pray please grant one wish
Before their time on earth is through
That they believe you died for them
So we can all be there with you

Hero

The battle raged carnage all around
Everywhere he looked men were going down
Soldiers were hit what should he do
Should he leave them there or see it through

He had the choice move ahead or run
It's likely no one would ever know
He could stay and help his brothers
Or turn his back on them and go

Turn and run away to save himself
Make that move and most likely he'd live
Move ahead to help his comrades
And a good chance his life he would give

In the chaos very few would ever see
The brave choice this soldier made
He ran into hell to save his friends
He made that choice and stayed

Comes a Time

Comes a time the kids seem to forget about you
All grown up now they live how they want to live
Hard as we try there's nothing we can do
Nothing we can say it is their time to give

Once upon a time it seems so long ago
They were so little and it was so good
And we sure do wish it still were so
If we could relive it surely we would

We have to face the fact those days are done
When they were ours just for you and me
Night and day they were our moon and sun
Those days are gone now it's time to let it be

Let's just be happy now for what we had
We were quite lucky you know it's true
Try to be happy turn away from the sad
God smiled very well upon me and you

Mother's Day

On this day that we reserve
For ones we love so true
I'd like to send a couple thoughts
Of what I think of you

You are the reason for my life
The one who helped me grow
And on this special day for you
I wanted you to know

That you'll be loved until the end
And after that for sure
My love for you will never die
Yes my love it will endure

Boy to Man

Boy to man in seven years
So much you've changed brings me to tears
The innocence of youth so fleeting
Into a shell find myself retreating

The boy we had has gone away
Though in our dreams he would have stayed
But just for us oh how selfish
In reality just our foolish wish

For the man that he has come to be
Much more a man much more than me
Not prouder could a father be
That he's become much more than me

Day by Day

It all came tumbling down that year
Nowhere to run nowhere to hide for me
Panic set in and suddenly nothing was clear
More than I could handle then it seemed to be

Thought I was doing OK and all seemed pretty good
Taking care of things at the time I thought were right
But the wall crashed down would change things if I could
Got really hard to get even a little sleep at night

Overwhelmed, so much at once, the pressure took its toll
End of the rope, the stress too much, I couldn't see
The toughest part was that I didn't have control
Thoughts inside too strong they had control of me

Then one night it came to me "don't let this stuff bother you"
"What good is that? You have to take things one by one"
"Take some deep breaths the air will help you get through"
The next morning darkness was replaced by morning sun

Where did they come from those words that freed me?
I'd like to say that I don't know but I'd be lying
The words without a doubt came from above now I see
Hard to explain some time ago I gave up trying

Heaven

Hand in hand left and right as far as I could see
Brilliant green hills below we soared through cloudless skies
Smiling and laughing how could this be?
Indescribable beauty I was seeing with surprise

Then it dawned on me that my life was through
I was in heaven then it occurred to me
So good to know what I believed was true
I was in heaven and now totally free

With so many people that I had known
Young and free now forever more
The ones that believed what God had shown
The faith we had pushed us on through the door

And yes I know that it's hard to believe
Nothing I can say no I cannot show you
Just look past this world and you can achieve
Yes you can get to that happy place too

You can get there too don't be afraid
Just believe and just open the door
You can get there too just lift up the shade
And you'll see eternal life forever more

To Marley Blue

A date on the calendar ... number 23
It's what we have in common ... You and me

Today is my birthday; be happy I'm told
But I think of you only; you'd be one month old.

We may never know why you were taken at birth
Perhaps you were just too good for this earth

I know you're an Angel and a bright "shining star"
So on each day 23 where ever you are ---

Look down on me and smile; and I will smile up at you
I love you and miss you; my sweet Marley Blue

Love; Grandma
(C. Hyler)

Final Gun

As he huddled up for one last time
And he stared into the ground
He knew his playing days were through
As the clock kept ticking down

He had known this game since he was young
And he had lived for every play
He worked so hard endured the pain
And he loved it all the way

And now he faced the final play
His last time in the sun
The ball was snapped; he played that play
Like it was his first one

As time went by he was blessed with a son
And as he grew his son wanted to play too
His dad taught him well and was there every step
His son said "dad I love this game just like you"

Now he stood and watched his young man's last play
And as the tears welled up in his eyes
The ball was snapped his son gave his all
His dad was so proud but he also realized

That this chapter was ending he knew it was so
He had done his best and had been there for his son
Now the time was now near to let it all go
The game they both loved was finally done

It's a Parent's War Too

Day after day you worry about him
Just like you did when he was young
Yes day after day you worry about him
But he's too far away nothing can be done

The days so long seem to last forever
But the nights are much longer you realize
The worry and fear that the word may come
Those endless nights hard to close your eyes

They want to kill your son and you know it
He's a main target yes it's sad to say
You lie awake; you know each coming day
Might be the day that he's taken away

And day after day you pray to God above
To protect him and bring him back to you
And after each day you're one day closer
One day closer to that dream coming true

If you're lucky the day comes you hold him in your arms
Yes he's a man but he'll always be your boy
Finally home for good you thank the Lord above
Endless nights replaced with endless joy

Everything to Me

I just want you to know
Before I have to go
I just want you to see
How much you mean to me

Always there for me
And I don't know why
You listened to me laugh
You listened to me cry

You didn't have to do that
You could have turned away
You didn't have to do that
You always chose to stay

My special one I hope you know
One of a kind and I love you so
You made my life I hope you see
You made my life you were everything to me

For Better or Worse

As I walked I came upon him
In a wheel chair he pushed his wife
Those vows they spoke so long ago
To them it meant for life

And though they had their ups and downs
Sometimes things; yes they did get tough
Those vows they spoke so long ago
Made the life they had good enough

For God had blessed them with a son
And a lovely daughter too
Those vows they spoke so long ago
Were enough because they knew

That God had smiled upon them
They were blessed in so many ways
Those vows they spoke so long ago
Meant for them until their final days

Always

I'm proud to be your dad you know
So blessed to have you near
It's hard for me to see you go
So good when you are here

And as you grow and as you change
I hope you'll always know
I'm here for you when you need me
I'll always love you so

Autumn

And then our son went off to school
Nothing would ever be the same
No one could have prepared us
For the emptiness and pain

And our daughter grew and she changed too
Like they do as they grow older
As autumn leaves fell to the ground
I knew that winter would feel colder

Final Glance

So haunted I can't get away
My mind is frozen to that day
I see her and that final glance
I'll never get another chance

To kiss her cheek and say goodbye
So hard to live I don't know why
The good die young or so it seems
Without the chance to live their dreams

And as I drove I tried to feel
The pain I'd know if this were real
I said a prayer for those that know
The unending loss that I fear so

And I pray to God to watch my dear
So I will always have her near
And let her see that life is good
Let it be long the way it should

Tommy Boy

The stone said Tommy and that was all
No date of birth or death
Why didn't it say when he was born?
Or the day of his last breath

I tried to picture Tommy Boy
How he laughed and how he cried
Was he happy with the life he had?
And what happened how he died

He did not have the silver spoon
And I know that he was poor
Judging by his simple stone
His family needed more

And did he have the brain to make
A difference in his world
If given time to use that gift
Before his life unfurled

Or was his life tough from the start
A life that wasn't fair
Was he given love from mom and dad?
Or did neither of them care .

How short was his time on this earth?
How come it doesn't say?
I guess for this forgotten boy
It's meant to be that way

Never Again

What you took from me that day
Cannot ever be returned
No longer can I trust again
That bridge forever burned

I thought about finding somebody new
But I knew that could never be
The risk I'd have to take for love
Was just not inside of me

I knew I couldn't bear to feel
That kind of pain again
The numbing hurt inside of me
Is the same as it was back then

I heard you found somebody new
And that makes me feel uneasy
With everything that we went through
How could you replace me?

So I've given up that part of me
My thoughts of someone new
I've given up that part of me
I have no need to replace you

Her Eyes

The sparkle in her eyes
I noticed right away
And much to my surprise
Found it hard to look away

Talking with her I learned
A caring mother all the way
And her children never doubt
That her love for them will stay

So sweet, so smart, so kind
And again to my surprise
Her inner beauty matched
The beauty of her eyes

And though she's far away
Sure as a new sun rise
My mind takes me back to
The sparkle in her eyes

Her Spot

She took her spot on the gym floor
On what would be her last full day
She laughed and played and had her fun
And then she went away

To read about the fire then
It made my heart just sink
I thought about that little girl
It really made me think

Life can be short life can be long
That's just the way it goes
The reason that it is that way
There is only one that knows

But if our lives were all the same
And we never saw such strife
How would we then appreciate
This gift that is our life

Come Out

"Come out of there" she said to him
But he never, ever did
Her little boy was trapped inside
His feelings always hid

She never heard "I love you mom"
Those words she longed to hear
She loved him but he always was
So far but yet so near

Every Time

Every time I look at you
I see you the same way
You look the way you looked to me
When we met on that first day

And everything I saw back then
I see when I see you
And everything I see I love
And that's why I love you

Soldier of God

As he grew up he never dreamed
That he'd be in this place
It went against what he was taught
This thing that he now faced

To make the choice to kill
Is what a warrior is trained to do
It's either you get him
Or surely he'll get you

Could he do what must be done?
To make it home alive
And no matter what choice he made
He felt his heart would not survive

So in the end he made the choice
The only one he could
The choice he made was the one
The Bible said he should

He laid his gun at his feet
And quickly it was done
He did what he truly believed
And met his chosen one

How I Wish

How I wish I could hold my kids again
When they were young and so new
One more time smell the freshness of their skin
And see that innocence so true

The softness of their skin like silk
That warmth and that tender touch
To cradle them and give them love
How I miss that so much

We provided every need they had
Always did the best that we could
To make them happy take away the sad
Loved them always the way we should

Those times they came those times they've gone
Sad to say that we can't go back there
But our memories yes they will go on
For the rest of our lives we can share

Inside My Dream

All was OK inside my dream
We could talk and listen again
And we laughed and cared and all was well
Like I remember way back when

The past was gone and we realized
What we had both done wasn't right
We laughed and forgave and all was good
And we held each other tight

Doing the dishes in my dream we were at ease
All the stress was no longer there
Arm and arm through the window we looked at the trees
The fresh spring breeze blowing in through our hair

We could talk again and it felt so nice
Like when we were young and free once again
We were happy and we cared once more
I think I saw a glimpse of heaven

Blue Skies

The skies are blue
The winds are light
When I think of you
My thoughts turn bright

You breathe fresh air into my heart
It makes me wish we weren't apart
When I think of you I feel alive
With you I know I can survive

Challenged

As they walked they helped each other
To decide what to do next
Should we go straight at the corner?
Or should we stop and take a left

The little things that we can do
For them it is so tough
But at least they have each other
So life isn't quite so rough

Faded Colors

She could not see what should be there
The colors all around
She could not see the happiness
The colors had turned brown

The world around her disappeared
Her love of life escaped
Her man had pulled his love away
It was more than she could take

Forever

I have found that you are there
So deep inside my heart
That even when you're not with me
We never are apart

It took some time for me to see
This love that is so true
Forever you are in my heart
And that's where I'll keep you

True Love

His love for her showed every day
And he loved her all he could
The years went by day after day
And he loved the way he should

She loved him more than words could say
She too loved the best she could
The years went by day after day
And she loved the way she should

They got the news one day they feared
That her life was near it's end
But even as the clock ticked down
Her love for him she still sent

And he was with her every step
For his life was dying too
But even as the clock ticked down
Inside of them they knew

That they had loved and they had lived
For each other every day
The love they had would never die
That their love would always stay

And he held her and he whispered things
What they'd seen and what they'd done
And when she took her final breath
They knew that they were one

Marty

He woke that day and never dreamed
That this would be the end
They asked the men for volunteers
And into the fire he went

To save the child that was inside
He never blinked an eye
And as he tried to save that kid
Our good friend Marty died

And Marty's dad he blamed himself
Because the son he loved was gone
For he had got Marty that job
Then everything went wrong

Although his son was hailed a hero
For what he did that day
His father's mind could not be changed
To look at it that way

Memorial Day

The flags fly low Memorial Day
To honor those that died
But all you think of is your son
How many times you've cried

For he was one who gave his life
So we could all be free
But every day you ask yourself
Why did this have to be?

There must have been a reason
For God to take this fine young man
We may not understand it
But I believe it's in his plan

All we can do is honor him
And hope that in the end
The tears you've cried forever dried
And you'll understand it then

From Above

She read him books from day to day
She taught him how to count
She made him happy in his play
She always was around

He grew into a gentle boy
Into a faithful man
She had been sent there from above
It was in God's whole plan

God Please

God please protect our children
When they're sleeping in the night
God please watch over our children
As they play in the daylight

Protect them and take care of them
Help them through life for me
If it's your will grant one more wish
Happy and long their lives will be

We

We live, we love, we rise, and we fall
And find out even through it all
That love is good and love is right
We should not quit without a fight

To find someone who makes us whole
To find someone although we know
Eventually the hurt will come
And we will lose our special one

And we will hurt and we will cry
We'll ask ourselves and wonder why
The one we loved had to go
We'll ask ourselves "why is it so?"

But in the end we'll know it's true
We had someone to help us through
And even though we risked the pain
Our lives must feel both sun and rain

So go for it don't sit and wait
Because if you don't and hesitate
You'll never know if you lost someone
Who may have been your morning sun

Because most of us want one who we
Can love and hold and helps us see
That love is good and love is right
We should not quit without a fight

Never

It can never be the way it was
Those special times back then
The only thing that we have left
Is to ask "do you remember when?"

If we could go back to those days
Would we do things differently?
The lessons that we've learned in life
Would the years have helped us see?

Or would the strain of work and life
That we lived through every day
Have been too much to overcome
Would we do things the same way?

We're only human so it's said
And we all do some things wrong
So if we could go back again
Would we write a different song?

One Last Time

They came together one last time
One last time as husband and as wife
She hoped that it would put an end
To all the anguish and the strife

But he never wanted it to end
And he never thought it would
He always thought it could be saved
He always thought it should

As the judge was reading to them both
That their marriage was at end
He wished that there was still a way
That he and her could still mend

Because what he felt inside his heart
A pain deep inside his chest
Was something that he could not bare
Watching his family laid to rest

Greener Grass

Your so called friends convinced you
The grass was greener somewhere else
You thought they cared about you
But they were thinking of themselves

They wanted one to run with
One to act just like they did
You couldn't see inside of them
The selfishness they hid

Grief

It never did let up for him
No matter where he went
The loss was too deep in his heart
No comfort ever sent

The pain was always with him
He just could not get away
It stayed with him until the end
Until his final day

Death Camp

They came in trains and never knew
Until it was too late
How could those people and their kids
Be doomed to such a fate

And how could he do that to them
Even though the orders came
Was he afraid that he would die?
That he'd be put to shame

Or did he fear that those he loved
If he failed to do the act
Would meet the same pathetic fate
That they too would be attacked

So he did what he was told to do
Though he knew it wasn't right
How hard it must have been for him
When he tried to sleep at night

To see their faces as they went
Knowing they would not return
The mothers and the kids they loved
Would die and then be burned

And when the war was dead and gone
Did he ever feel alive?
To know because he did his job
Not one of them survived

Or would a bullet to his head
Have been easier to bear
Than the hell that he is living now
All the guilt he cannot share

Poverty

He walked the street in filthy pants
And his face showed only pain
If he'd been given half the chance
But in his life he saw only rain

And even though I don't have much
He would be rich if he were in my shoes
But the life he had was only such
That he was born to only lose

He loved his wife and children
So I'm sure it hurt for him to know
This was the life he could give them
And he knew it would always be so

He probably couldn't pay the rent
You could almost sense it in his mood
On top of that it was probably true
That he could barely buy them food

Scholar

When he was young it could be seen
That he was something rare
And early on he had that drive
A thirst beyond compare

And as he grew his mom helped him
To learn everything he could
He was lucky she was there
Just like a good mom should

He's never lost his love for learning
And I'm sure he never will
Now he's at the highest place
Learning all that he can still

And he may teach someday I think
His knowledge he will share
To other ones who just like him
Have a thirst beyond compare

Her Babies

She loved her babies oh so well
She kissed their owies when they fell
When it was time to go to sleep
Her babies knew her love was deep

And as they grew she did her best
To put their worries all to rest
Now look how good they have become
She is the reason she was the one

Her Knight

Her pain was overwhelming
To find what he had done
Her knight in shining armor
Had rode into the sun

But her love it would not leave her
Because she knew like a new day
He would be coming back to her
He would come home to stay

So Good

When no one else was good to me
I could always count on you
You didn't have to be so nice
But you were and you helped me get through

The times I thought I had reached the end
I wondered why you would care about me
It was the kindness you didn't need to send
Helped me to live you helped me to see

That for all the mean and thoughtless ones
There are good ones out there like you
Before my time was up and my life was done
You showed me for sure that it was true

You know I never will forget you dear
You are so sweet you are so true
In my heart I will always hold you near
I am forever indebted to you

Hugging You

When I hug you dear I can't let go
That's how much I love you
To feel you tight inside my arms
Is what I want to do

And though we cannot stay that way
For hours at a time
When it comes to hugging you my dear
A little works just fine

Her Little Boy

Her little Boy was only three
The day her life turned gray
To tell her it was meant to be
She just couldn't see it that way

He was her sun he was her moon
The light of her whole life
The day her son was taken
Was the end of his mom's life

Some Day

How cruel the world why must it be
Why can't we live in harmony?
Open your eyes and you can see
The depth of human cruelty

The world we have such a big place
More than enough for the human race
All people could be fed starvation replaced
Could put a smile on everybody's face

But there are some that just don't care
About the dying, sickness, and such despair
They cheat the world and don't play fair
More for themselves why would they share?

But maybe someday we all will see
All eyes will open see how things should be
That life isn't only always just about me
There is plenty here for all humanity

I'm Sorry

The words I spoke that hurt you so
I'd like to take them back
And ask forgiveness for their pain
I'm so sorry for my attack

I wanted you to also feel
My hurt that was so strong
To make you hurt because I hurt
I'm sorry I was wrong

I Miss

I miss those little wiggly hands
I miss those wiggly toes
I miss them playing in the sand
I miss that little nose

I miss those days and I miss those nights
I miss hugging and I miss touch
I miss their laughter in the house
I miss them oh so much

So Young

In a hospital bed so young so new
So scared and so alone
There's nothing they can do for her
But she won't be able to go home

How fair is life to this sweet girl
When it starts and then it's done
I'd like to know please tell me how
This happens to one so young

No high school prom or college days
No thrill of that first kiss
How fair is this to one so pure
All the fun in life she'll miss

But I trust that God has made a place
Where she'll play, she'll laugh, she'll be loved
To give her what she's lost down here
Yes I believe it's there above

Mickey

He was the best there ever was
To him no one compared
But when his time was running out
The people stopped and stared

The one who had it all it seemed
Had only a short time left to live
The love his family should have felt
Now it was too late for him to give

Just Like That

And just like that she came to me
It's crazy but it's true
Someone as perfect as can be
I can't believe it's you

If I could close my eyes and wish
For one to be with me
I'd open them and she'd be you
You'd be the one I'd see

Thankful

A mother lies in anguish
As her new born baby dies
As cancer take their teenage son
His parents kneel and cry

A phone call comes late in the night
With the words that we all dread
There's been a nasty accident
And someone we love is dead

So how can I feel sadness?
For what's happened in my life
I've never felt the pain they've felt
Much more cutting than a knife

So I'm thankful for each day I have
When I don't have that pain
Because any second it could change
And then I would feel the same

Light of My Life

You are the sun that lights my life
I just wanted you to know
And when I see you every day
My feelings start to glow

I like the way you make me feel
Your warm and tender touch
Your love for me brings happiness
You help me feel so much

Looking Back

There's nothing wrong with looking back
With living in the past
The memories of those golden years
How I hope they'll always last

What good is it to look ahead?
When I know it won't compare
To those golden years with our children
How I wish I still were there

Thank You Lord

Thank you Lord for giving us
All the time we had with them
Thank you Lord you've helped us see
How precious those moments had been

We miss those days and those nights
And we wish that we still could be there
At least we saw their play and fights
We have memories that we can still share

We would not trade the times we had
For all the gold that we ever would need
For what is gold compared to that?
It is worthless you have to concede

The missing them yet while so sad
So invaluable it was now we know
The golden memories of what we had
At least in our minds they will go

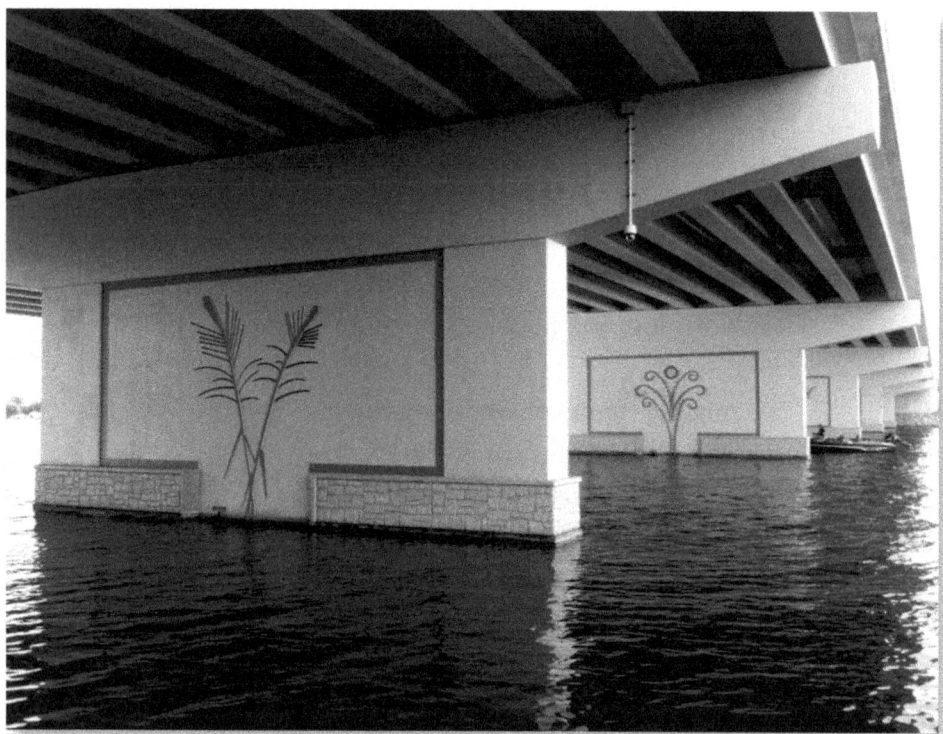

Thank You River

I need to Thank You River
For all the joy you've given me
When my daughter took those fish from you
The look on her face was something to see

It meant everything to see her face
Thank you for that gift that you gave me
To see her now in such a happy place
Thank you for what you have saved me

I need to Thank You River
That you were there for her and me
And I need to Thank You River
For all the fun that you've let us see

It meant everything to see her smile
Now as I watch the rain falling on you
As I gaze at the wall and look for a while
Happy pictures of my daughter I view

My Light

I have a light still in my life
Someone who helps me live
Sometimes she doesn't seem to care
But most times her love she gives

Those times my daughter opens up
Are just enough to help me see
It helps me know my life has worth
Yes my daughter still needs me

Only Love

It's only love I'm feeling now
No anger, hurt, or pain
It's only sunshine that I see
No longer does it rain

I had to let those feelings go
They were no good you see
I had to lay them all to rest
They were no good for me

The Message

The Plan was set
I had not confided
The when and how
It had been decided

Kissed her goodbye and drove away
Knowing I would not return
For this would be my final day
That my car would crash and burn

But then a call that never came
All those years for the first time
She was at home sick and alone
Out of my hole then I had to climb

And I realized that God had sent
A message through her from above
That it was not time for me to go
Through my daughter came His love

One Click

You're just one click away from them
Just one genetic tweak
Next time you want to ridicule
Please think before you speak

Yes things would be much different
If you'd been born inside that place
Then you would see things through their eyes
All the obstacles that they face

One More Day

And if I had just one more day
If somehow that I knew
My wish would be for my last day
To spend it all with you

To kiss your face and hold you close
Say I love you one last time
Would be my one and only wish
I would want for all time

The Lot

She pulled into the parking lot
And her hands went to her face
She thought she was there all alone
That the lot was a safe place

But I happened to be working then
And I couldn't help but think
What was it that caused such pain?
What had caused her heart to sink?

I thought and then made up my mind
I began to walk to her to see
If there was something I could do
But her hand had turned the key

And as she drove that van away
I knew then that I'd never know
What caused her to stop in the lot?
What it was that hurt her so

Raging Waters

The raging waters disappeared
No longer did he need to run
The storm that stirred his troubled soul
Saved by a brilliant sun

And now the boat it sails the sea
A calm harbor always near
The storm that hurt him never comes
And now he has no fear

Red Drapes

As she told me what they meant to her
Those red drapes in that place
The pain flowed from her broken heart
I could see it on her face

The one she missed with all her soul
Her daughter that she loved
Had died of cancer in that room
Where those red drapes still hanged above

To My Children

Despite the cold reality
Just cannot bring myself to see
That what it is will be will be
I cannot change what's destiny

But in my dreams if I could say
Could make a plan could chart your way
I know the thing that I would do
The things that I would wish for you

That you would live a life that's long
A life of happiness and full of song
You'd be happy with the life you had
A life of love with very little sad

Although I cannot have my way
There's something that I'd like to say
That I will pray until my end
My dreams for you that God will send

No One

No one can take the place of him
I'm sorry but it's true
You have to try to let him go
Before your life is through

For he would want you to be free
To find somebody new
Because he loved you like he did
That's what he'd want for you

Not My Last Goodbye

The hardest thing I'll have to do
Is say my last goodbye to you
I hope through everything you see
That you have meant the world to me

With everything that we went through
You were always there I could count on you
And the beautiful place where I hope to go
More beautiful when you join me I hope it's so

Warm Spring Rain

The years flew by yes time went fast
I thought those care free days would last
But through it all happiness and pain
I always lived for that warm spring rain

The good the bad yeah I made it through
I did my best what else can you do
But through it all despite the strain
I always lived for that warm spring rain

To cleanse me and to make me feel
That I am young again as if it were real
My youth I know I can't regain
But I'll always live for that warm spring rain

That warm spring rain just a few more years
Is all I hope for there will be no more tears
But through it all I will not restrain
I always lived for that warm spring rain

The Fence

The pain of life had taken its toll
His loss of love intense
He had to look inside his soul
He had to cross the fence

And on the other side he found
That there was another way
He had to keep his children safe
He finally chose to stay

The Light

I saw a light that warmed my heart
And I didn't know what to do
I felt the need to laugh and cry
Because I knew my life was through

Now all the pain that I had felt
Was replaced with only love
And I knew that I was home at last
Surrounded by God's love

What Happened?

What happened to the world I knew?
So innocent and oh so free
I ran and played and had my fun
Thought that's the way it always would be

But as time went by I began to see
That life wasn't just games and fun
The world that had been so fun for me
Had some clouds it was not only sun

The more I grew and the more I learned
Innocence and feeling free passed away
I realized that the things that I yearned
Forever gone that's the way it would stay

What happened to the world I knew?
So innocent, so free, and so right
I'm afraid the truth for me and you
Far less sun now mixed in with some night

When I Look Back

When I look back on my life if I could live it over
What would I change if I could do it all again?
Would I go from start to finish clean and sober?
Or keep on doing what I've done until the end

When I look at the poor people that I'd surely see
Would I try to change and think of them instead?
Would I try to take the wrongs and make them right?
Do things the same keep on looking straight ahead

Would I still ignore the things that should be changed?
What would I do if I had knowledge and could see?
Would I try to change some things to make a difference?
Or would I just think about myself and let it be

Would I have the courage to try to make things better?
Would I choose a different path see what I find
Would the risk that it would take make me a coward?
Or would I have the guts to say what's on my mind

Too Worried

I was too worried about myself
And I shouldn't have been that way
I was so worried about myself
That I forgot to pray

For those that matter in my life
The ones that care for me
I was too worried about myself
That I forgot to see

Your Heart

You gave your heart to him plus more
He knew you loved him so
And as the end was drawing near
You knew he had to go

Remember that you did your best
And he knew that he was loved
And you will be with him again
Together up above

When My Time Has Come

We'll never know when our time has come
To head back to the place where we came from
I hope I'm ready when I go that way
I hope I'm ready on my final day

I've seen some the things I wanted to see
Tried to be good to those who cared for me
When I leave I hope I have few regrets
When I leave and take that final step

Will I be happy with what I've left behind?
When I move forward to see what I find
Beyond this earthly time will I see?
I'm ready for what's ahead of me

I hope that God then chooses me
So forever more I will be free
Will I find that I'm worthy to go on in?
That a new life for me is set to begin?

Your Special Smile

The times I see you smile at me
Is when I feel my best
Your smile makes me feel good inside
And puts my heart to rest

You are the sunshine in my life
The one that keeps me warm
And when I see you smile at me
I can weather any storm

Why

I saw that picture torn apart
It had meant so much to me
Those pieces could have been my heart
Why be so mean to me

Because we had lived and we had loved
As husband and as wife
To rip my heart to pieces now
You should have used a knife

The Promise

You never left my heart he cried
As he held her and he wept
He said he'd be there at the end
A promise that he now kept

The years they lost never replaced
The hurt they couldn't forget
As he kissed her cheek and said goodbye
His love was with her yet

The Question

Why did you do the thing you did
That caused him to take his life?
And were you ready to take care
Of his children and his wife?

Before you did that selfish thing
You really should have thought
Of all the lives that would be changed
When you and her got caught

Innocent Souls

Innocent souls too young to sway
So young and naive that's for sure
I wish they all could just stay that way
Too innocent to know what life has in store

If they just could stay the way they are
Keep their head clear without looking around
Stay young and free only look to the stars
If Innocent souls could ignore the sounds

And keep that feeling not questioning why
Eyes not seeing the bad that's all around them
Ears unable to hear those chaotic cries
Feeling inside how they felt up until then

I know they say innocence is so fleeting
But for their sake if it skipped a turn or two
Would the cycle then stop or keep repeating?
Would it be better is what I'm asking you?

The Last Thing You Write

The last one you write should be your best
Say so much more than all the rest
Those final words should say the most
And should surely include a final toast

To all you've seen and all you've done
Kind words to cover everyone
That had an impact on your life
Were there for you through good and strife

The last one you write should fittingly
Tell those you loved to help them see
That they were special above the rest
They made you feel that you were blessed

That they made your life a special time
A flowing gift so full of rhyme
And thank them for the love they shared
It meant so much that they had cared

www.ingramcontent.com/pod-product-compliance
Lightning Source LLC
Chambersburg PA
CBHW071834020426
42331CB00007B/1730